Draw and Color
Animals

Learn to draw and color 26 wild
creatures, step by easy step,
shape by simple shape!

Illustrated by Diana Fisher

Getting Started

When you **look** closely at the **drawings** in this book, you'll notice that they're made up of basic shapes, such as circles, triangles, and rectangles. To draw all your wild kingdom favorites, just start with simple shapes as you see here. It's easy and fun!

Circles are great for drawing heads, chests, and hips.

Ovals are good for drawing animals' bodies.

Triangles are often best for drawing beaks, ears, and hooves.

Coloring Tips

There's more than one way to bring your **animal pals** to life on paper—you can use crayons, markers, or colored pencils. Just be sure you have plenty of good natural colors—black, brown, and gray, plus yellow, orange, red, and green.

Pencil

Colored pencil

Crayon

Marker

Aardvark

The aardvark has a **long** nose, sharp claws, and small, **beady** eyes. It first smells and then digs out its meals of ants and termites.

1
2
3
4
5

6

Emu

The emu's **fluffy** plumage hides its small **wings.** But its tall, thin legs allow this flightless bird to run up to 30 miles per hour!

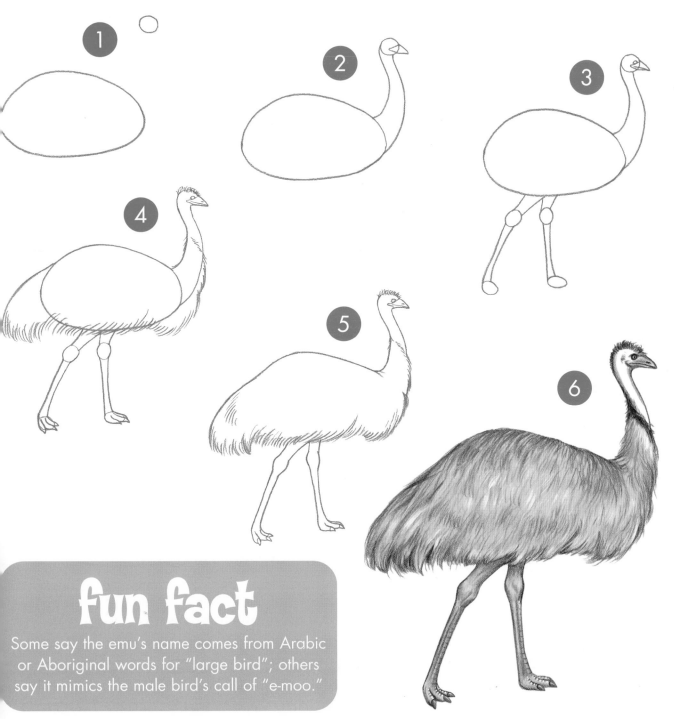

fun fact

Some say the emu's name comes from Arabic or Aboriginal words for "large bird"; others say it mimics the male bird's call of "e-moo."

High Risk

Giant Panda

In China the **barrel-shaped** panda is called "baixiong" ("white bear"), but the black markings give this animal a two-toned look.

fun fact

The giant panda has a very limited diet—it survives almost entirely on bamboo! It eats the shoots of this grasslike plant in the spring, leaves in the summer, and stems in the winter.

5

6

High Risk
The panda is at high risk for extinction; its kind (or *species*) is *endangered*. There are very few giant pandas alive in the wild today.

7

Polar Bear

The cuddly-looking polar bear has a **large**, round, **furry** body—but this cutie hunts and devours seals, walruses, and even whales!

1

2

3

4

5

At Risk
The population of polar bears decreases every day. Efforts must be made to save the bear and its Arctic home to prevent extinction.

Cheetah

With its **long,** powerful legs; **lean,** muscular body; and stylish, spotted coat, you might say the cheetah is a hunter "dressed to kill"!

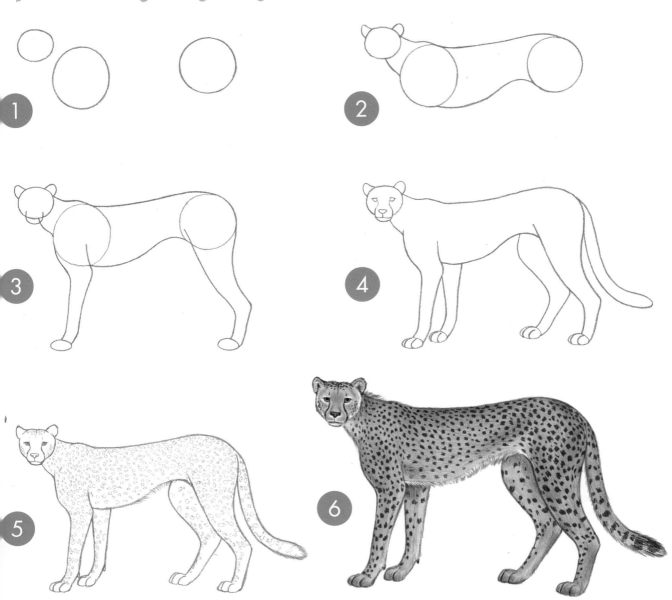

fun fact

Sure, the cheetah is quick—it can reach speeds of more than 60 mph, making it the fastest animal in the world. But this big cat can maintain its top speed only for short bursts. After 10–12 seconds of running, the cheetah begins to overheat.

Elephant

One of the **largest** beasts of the **animal** kingdom, an African elephant has a thick trunk, big legs, long tusks, and giant ears!

1

2

3

fun fact

The elephant is known for its great memory—but why? One reason is the elephant has an enormous brain! Weighing in at around 12 pounds, it's the largest and heaviest mammal brain. (The human brain weighs only about 3 pounds.)

4

5

6

High Risk

The African elephant is an endangered animal. It has a very high chance of becoming extinct in the next 20 years.

Tiger

Every **big cat** has a large head and rounded ears. But a tiger also has camouflaging stripes that help this stand-out cat blend in!

1

2

3

4

6

5

fun fact

A tiger usually eats about 15–35 pounds of meat per feeding, dining on deer, pigs, cattle, monkeys, birds, reptiles, and even fish. And when it's really hungry, a tiger can eat up to 90 pounds of meat in one meal!

Toucan

It's hard to ignore the **keel-billed** toucan's **beak!** It's almost as long as the bird's body—and it features a rainbow of colors.

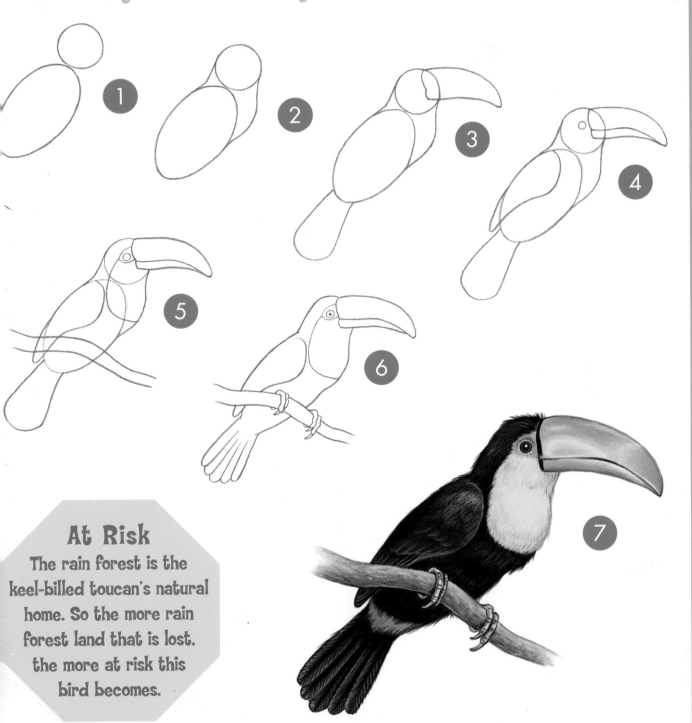

At Risk
The rain forest is the keel-billed toucan's natural home. So the more rain forest land that is lost, the more at risk this bird becomes.

13

Giraffe

With its **lanky** legs and long neck, the **towering** giraffe rises above the competition to claim the title of "tallest animal on Earth."

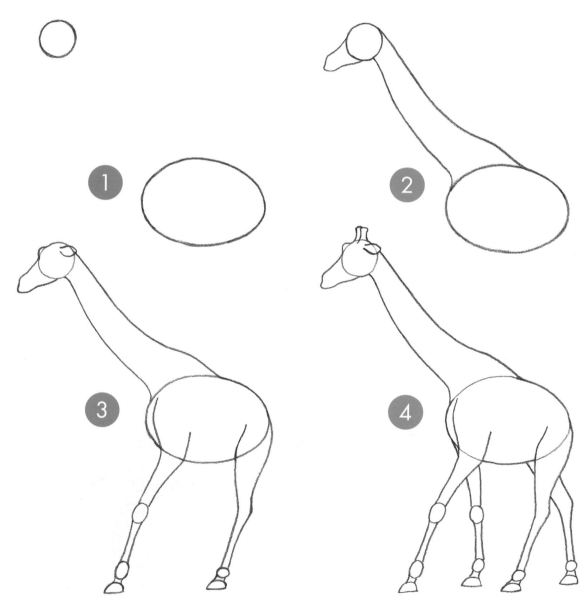

fun fact
A baby giraffe, called a "calf," can stand up on its own about 20 minutes after it's born! And, at birth, a giraffe calf already measures about 6-1/2 feet tall!

Wildebeest

The wildebeest—or gnu—looks **big** and **broad** with high shoulders and a humped back, but it prances away from danger on four skinny legs!

1
2
3
4
5
6

Low Risk
There are about 18,000 gnus in the world. Most live in protected areas. This animal's population is growing, so it's at low risk of extinction.

Crocodile

Start this drawing with a thin **oval** body and a small **round** head—then add the crocodile's long, strong tail and big, powerful jaws!

fun fact Can't tell the difference between the crocodile and the alligator? Check out the snout. The crocodile's snout is longer and V-shaped; the alligator's snout is wider and U-shaped.

Hippopotamus

"Massive" is a good start for describing this **round,** hulking beast! A full-grown hippo can weigh up to 1-1/2 tons.

1

2

3

4

5

6

Animals in the Wild

Each animal has a **natural environment,** or *habitat*— whether a desert, forest, or water. To realistically portray your favorite animals, draw them in their own wild habitat, like this African grassland!

Kangaroo

Low Risk

With a **thick,** powerful tail, **strong** hind legs, and huge rear feet, you can identify the kangaroo from a hop, skip, and a jump away!

fun fact

For male kangaroos, kick boxing isn't a sport; it's a way of life. When fighting over mates, food, and resting spots, kangaroos will lock arms with each other, lean on their tails, and kick. The first kangaroo to get pushed over loses.

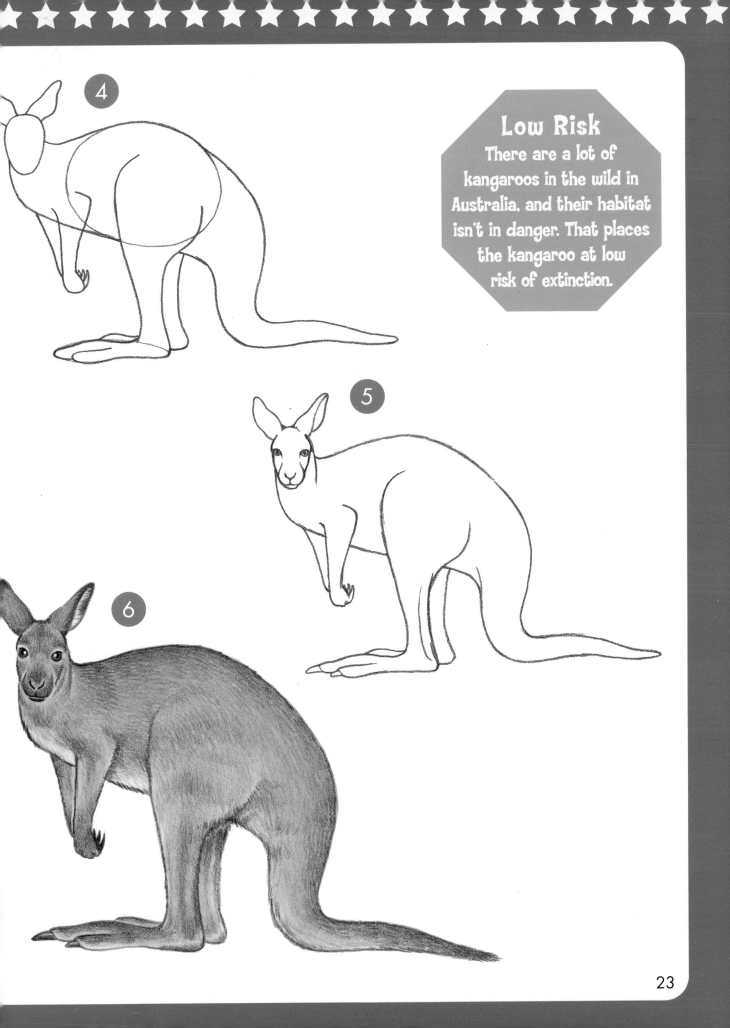

4

5

6

Koala

This soft, **woolly** tree-dweller suspends its **short,** round body by clinging to eucalyptus trees—both its home and its food.

Lemur

Although its **long**, curving tail is the **ring-tailed** lemur's most striking feature, this animal is also known for its graceful, catlike posture.

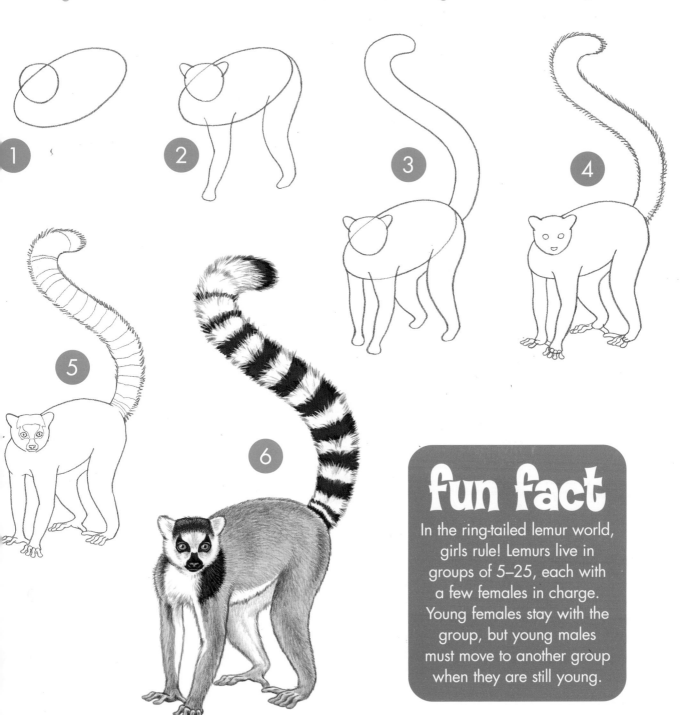

fun fact

In the ring-tailed lemur world, girls rule! Lemurs live in groups of 5–25, each with a few females in charge. Young females stay with the group, but young males must move to another group when they are still young.

25

Spider Monkey

Black-handed spider monkeys are **small** and **thin**. Their hands, feet, and heads are black, and black masks frame their round eyes.

fun fact

This monkey gets its name from its long, spidery limbs—all five of them! The spider monkey's tail is as long and as strong as its arms and legs. And the tail's hairless tip makes it easier for the monkey to tightly grasp branches or food!

Low Risk

The black-handed spider monkey has a thriving population, even though about 70% of its Central American habitat has been lost.

7

8

9

10

Komodo Dragon

Don't let its **draggin'** belly fool you—the **large**, wrinkled, prehistoric-looking Komodo dragon is a swift runner and a fast climber.

High Risk

The natural habitat of the Komodo dragon is a group of four small islands in Indonesia. There are only about 5,000 Komodos in the wild today.

Armadillo

Oddly enough, the "nine-banded" armadillo can have from 8 to 10 bands around its body, making its tough armor more flexible.

fun fact

Many mammals give birth to multiple young, but only the nine-banded armadillo regularly produces them all from a single egg. The female nine-banded armadillo always gives birth to quadruplets—that's four identical baby armadillos.

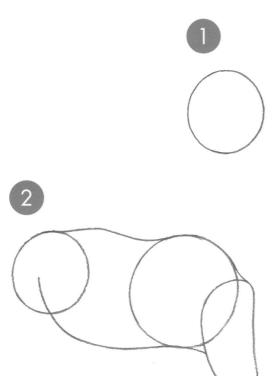

High Risk

Rhinoceros

The **short** legs of this white rhino support its **bulky** body, and it uses its two curved, triangular-shaped horns to dig food and defend itself!

fun fact

Why name a gray rhino "white"? Blame it on a misunderstanding. The Dutch word for wide—*weit*—is pronounced "white." *Weit* was meant to describe the rhino's wide, square muzzle—not its color. It's no coincidence that this animal is also called the "square-lipped" rhino.

5

High Risk
In Africa, the white rhino population suffers due to habitat loss. But illegal hunting (called "poaching") is also a threat to this rhino's survival.

6

7

Platypus

It may have a **duck's bill** and webbed feet, but the platypus's flat tail and velvety, waterproof coat are all its own!

1

2

3

4

5

6

fun fact

The platypus isn't psychic, but it does have ESP—extra sensory perception! In addition to using sight, sound, taste, smell, and touch, the platypus can sense tiny electrical signals with its snout, helping it find food underwater.

7

Orangutan

Every orangutan has a **bare** face, **round** eyes, and small ears, but only the male has large, round cheek pads and a long, hairy beard.

High Risk
Orangutans have three threats to deal with in Asia: habitat loss, hunters, and kidnappers! Orangutans are sold both as meat and as pets.

Tapir

What's **black** and **white** with a long curved snout? The Malayan tapir! This "living fossil" has looked exactly the same for 30 million years

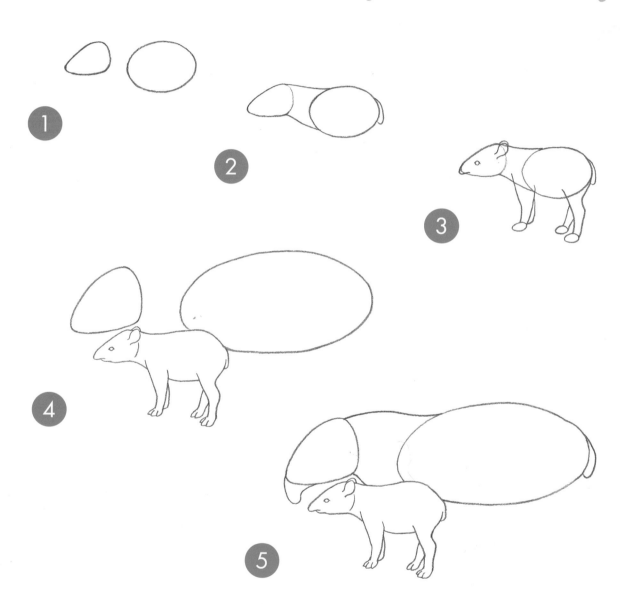

1

2

3

4

5

fun fact

Every tapir is born with spots and stripes. This camouflage pattern protects the young tapir from predators, helping it blend in with vegetation. The "broken" coloration of the adult Malayan tapir also acts as camouflage.

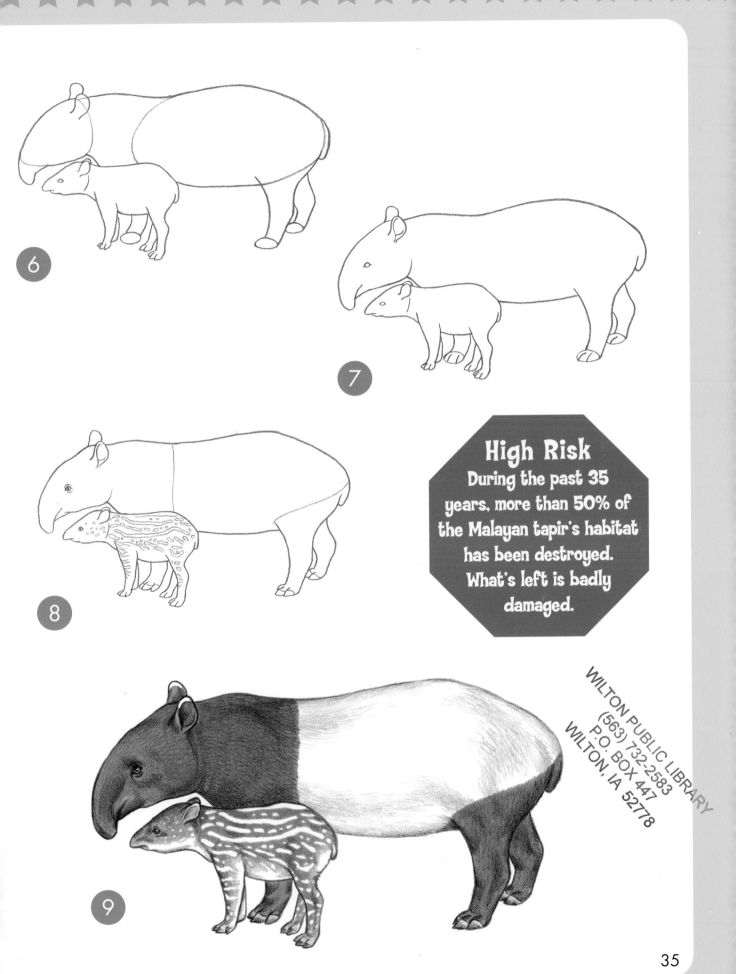

6

7

High Risk
During the past 35 years, more than 50% of the Malayan tapir's habitat has been destroyed. What's left is badly damaged.

8

9

Hyena

The **spotted** hyena has many **doglike** features, but its large rounded ears and sloping back give this animal a unique appearance.

1

2

3

4

5

6

7

Wombat

Featuring a **compact** body, **stocky** limbs, and a pointed snout, the wombat looks kind of like a small bear crossed with a pig!

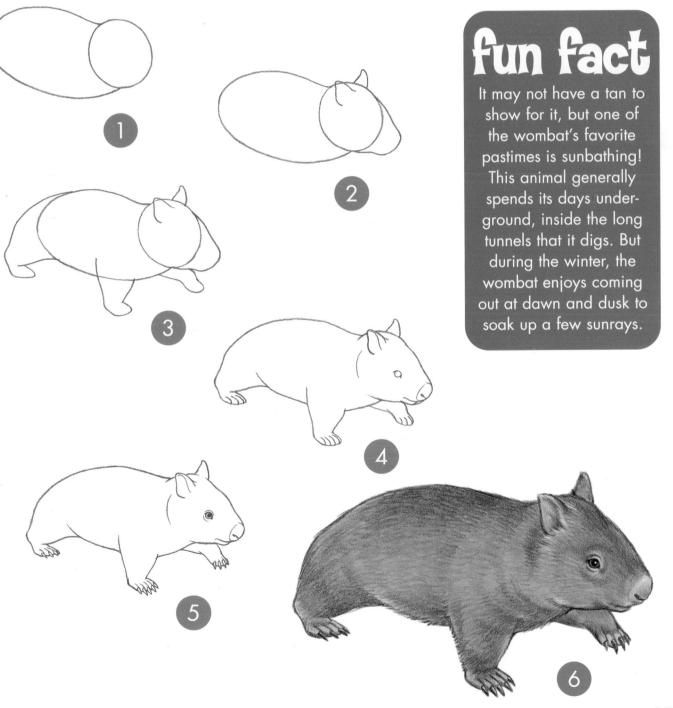

fun fact

It may not have a tan to show for it, but one of the wombat's favorite pastimes is sunbathing! This animal generally spends its days underground, inside the long tunnels that it digs. But during the winter, the wombat enjoys coming out at dawn and dusk to soak up a few sunrays.

Okapi

Its **stripes** make the okapi look like a zebra, but this **tall,** two-toned animal has the long legs and flexible neck of a giraffe.

At Risk
The okapi is quickly losing its habitat to human farms, roads, and homes. And this animal is also hunted as a source of food.

fun fact

The Okapi lives only in the tropical forests of northeastern Zaire, on the African continent, where it hides itself in the thick vegetation. A very shy animal, the okapi is rarely seen in the wild. Because of this, the okapi was thought to be a "forest zebra" until 1900, when it was finally recognized as its own unique species of animal. The okapi has no relation to the zebra, but it is the only known relative of the giraffe.

Zebra

From its **black** muzzle to the tips of its **long** ears, the zebra's face is covered in narrow stripes; its body and mane have broader stripes

fun fact

Experts aren't exactly sure why zebras have stripes, but they think that the markings serve some sort of purpose. The stripes might help the animals recognize other members of their herd, regulate temperature, or even confuse predators.

Produced by the creative team at Walter Foster Publishing, Inc.
(and inspired by the team's favorite animals):

Sydney J. Sprague, Publisher (Elephant)
David Rosemeyer, Art Director (Emu)
Barbara Kimmel, Managing Editor (Zebra)
Jenna Winterberg, Project Editor (Okapi)
Elizabeth Runyen, Association Project Editor (Orangutan)
Toni Gardner, Production Manager (Tiger)
Anne Jacobs, Production Controller (Gnu)
Lawrence Marquez, Production Coordinator (Toucan)
Monica Noemi Mijares DeCuir, Production Artist (Cheetah)
Shirley Samarin, Production Artist (Wombat)

Illustrated by Diana Fisher (Tapir)

Walter Foster Publishing, Inc.
23062 La Cadena Drive, Laguna Hills, California 92653
www.walterfoster.com

Printed in China.